Give Same COLOR A Thumbs Up

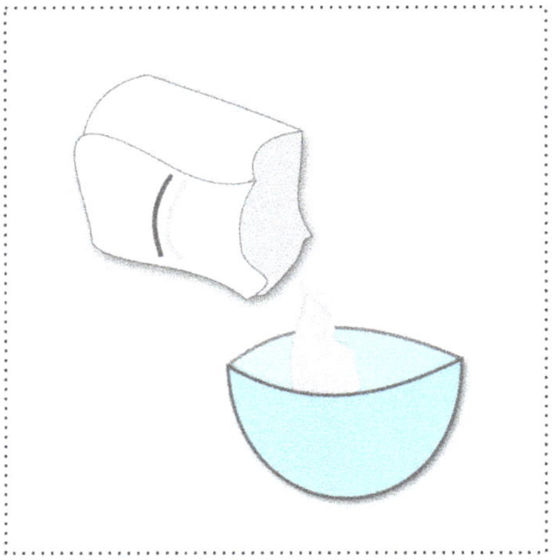

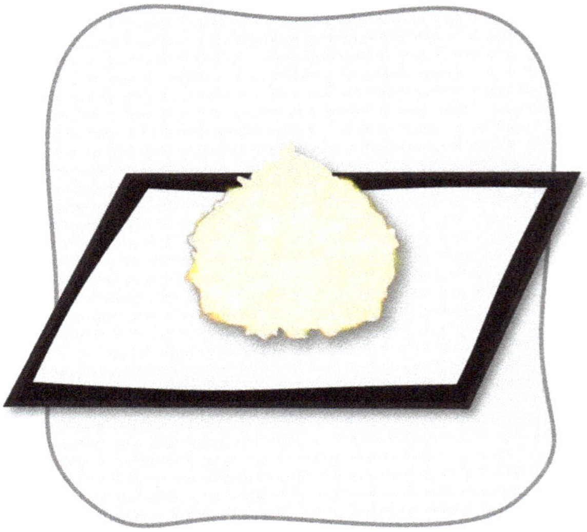

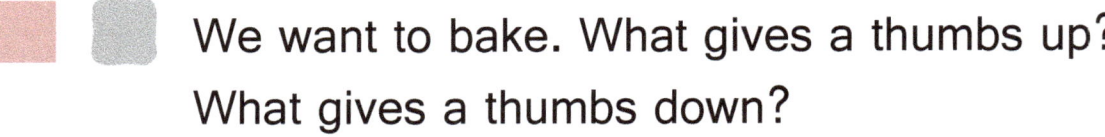 We want to bake. What gives a thumbs up? What gives a thumbs down?

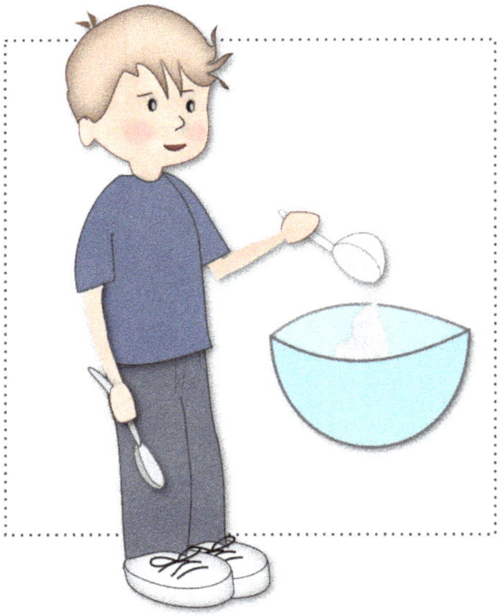

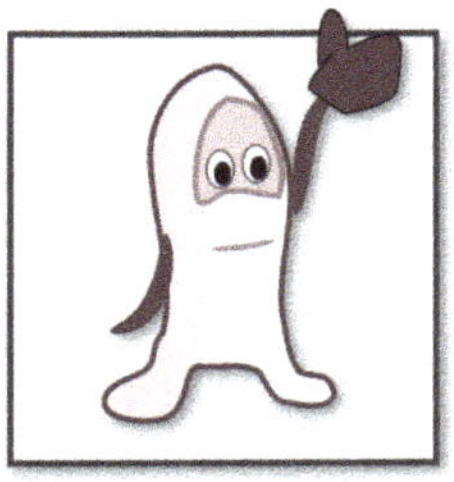

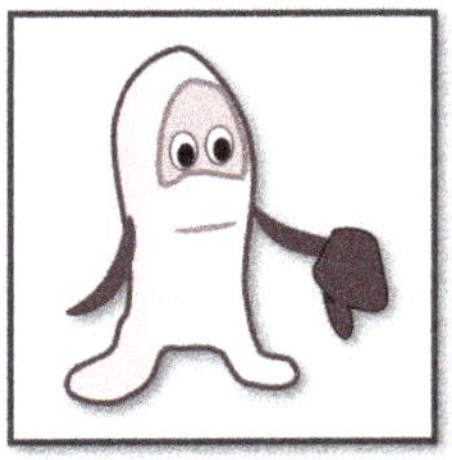

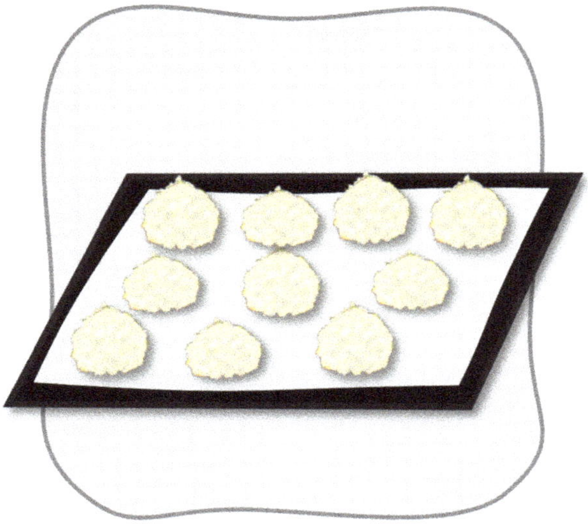

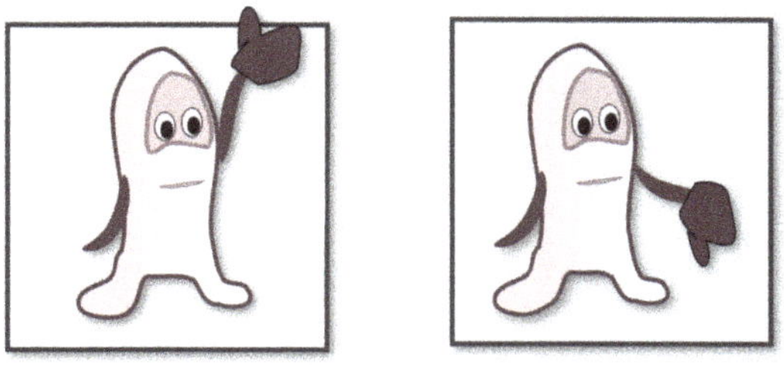

We want to bake. What should we ... bring out? Mix with? Use to bake the cookies? Give a thumbs up!

 We want to bake. What should we bring out?
Give a thumbs up ... or down.

 We want to bake. What should we bring out?
Give a thumbs up ... or down.

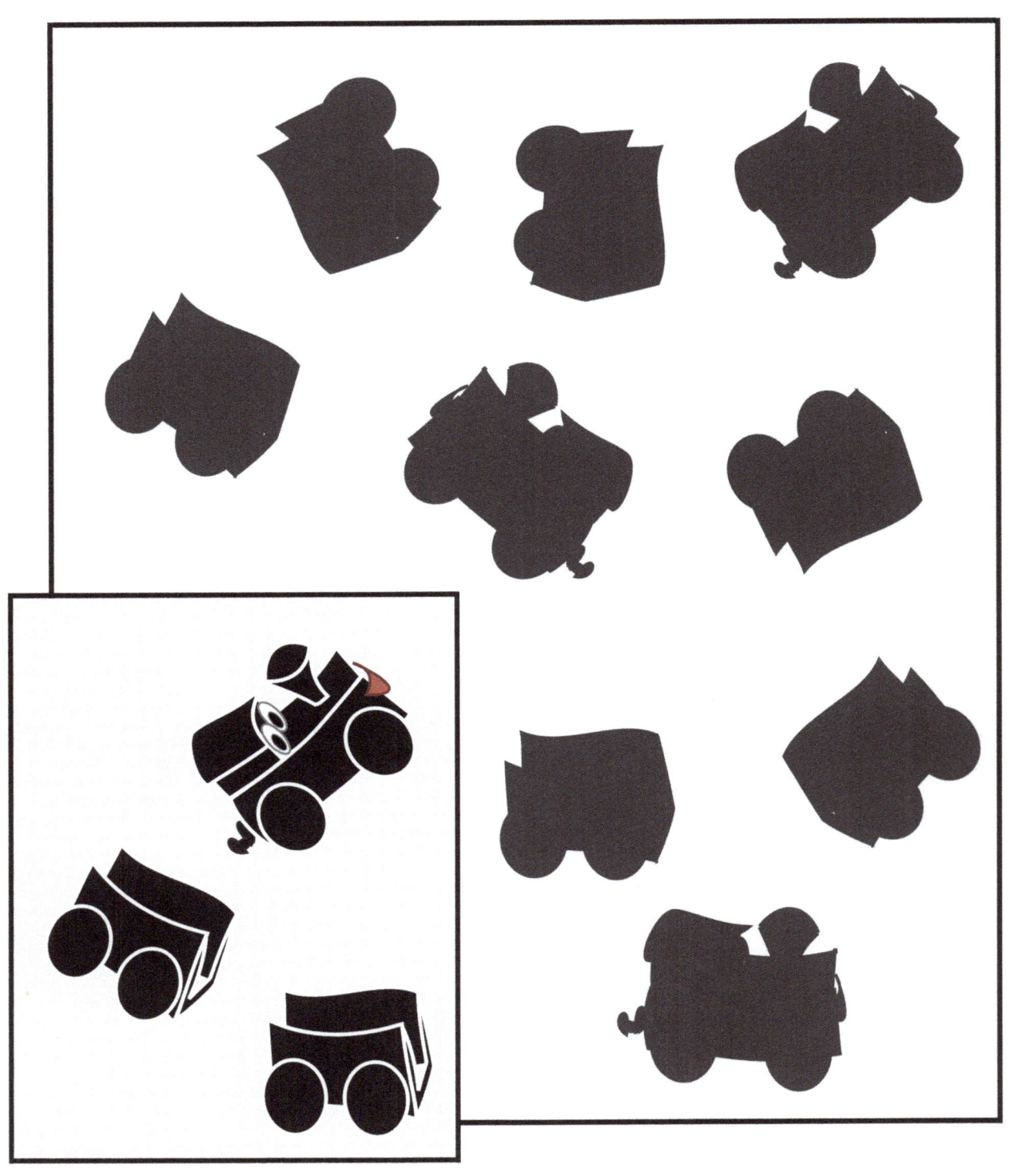

Find 3 Same

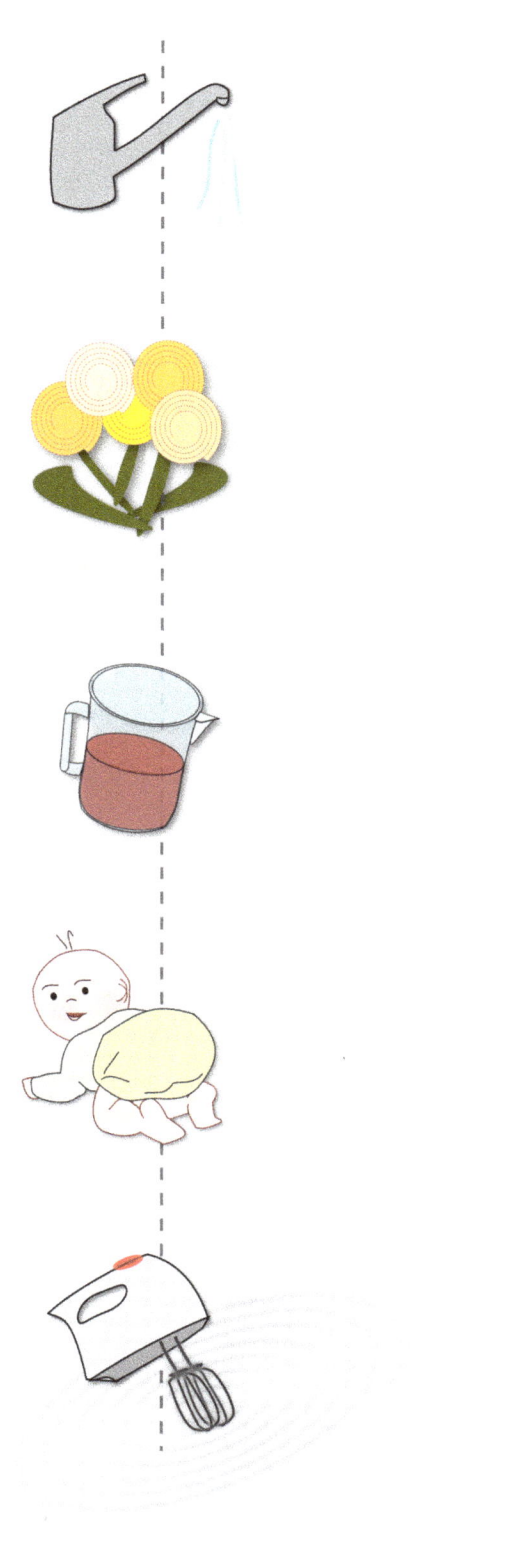
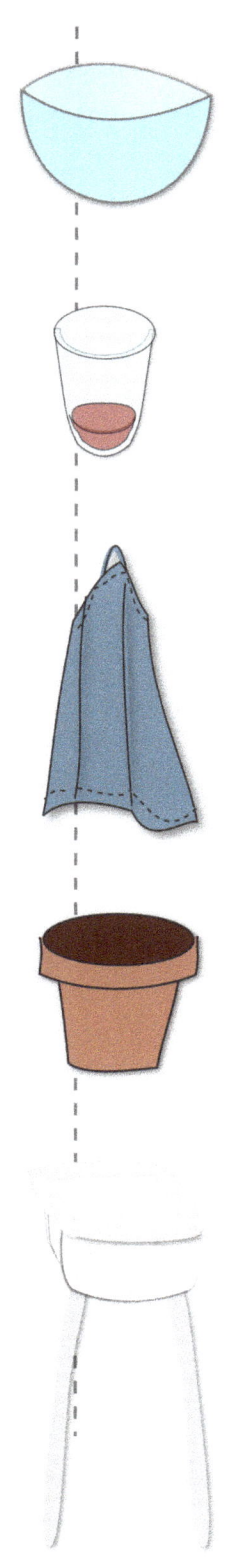

 What goes together? Why do we need it?

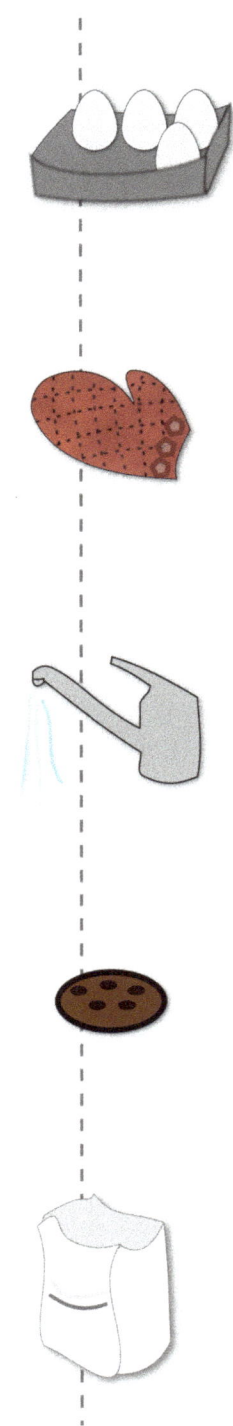

 What goes together? Why do we need it?

Super-A wants to bake. Find what she needs!

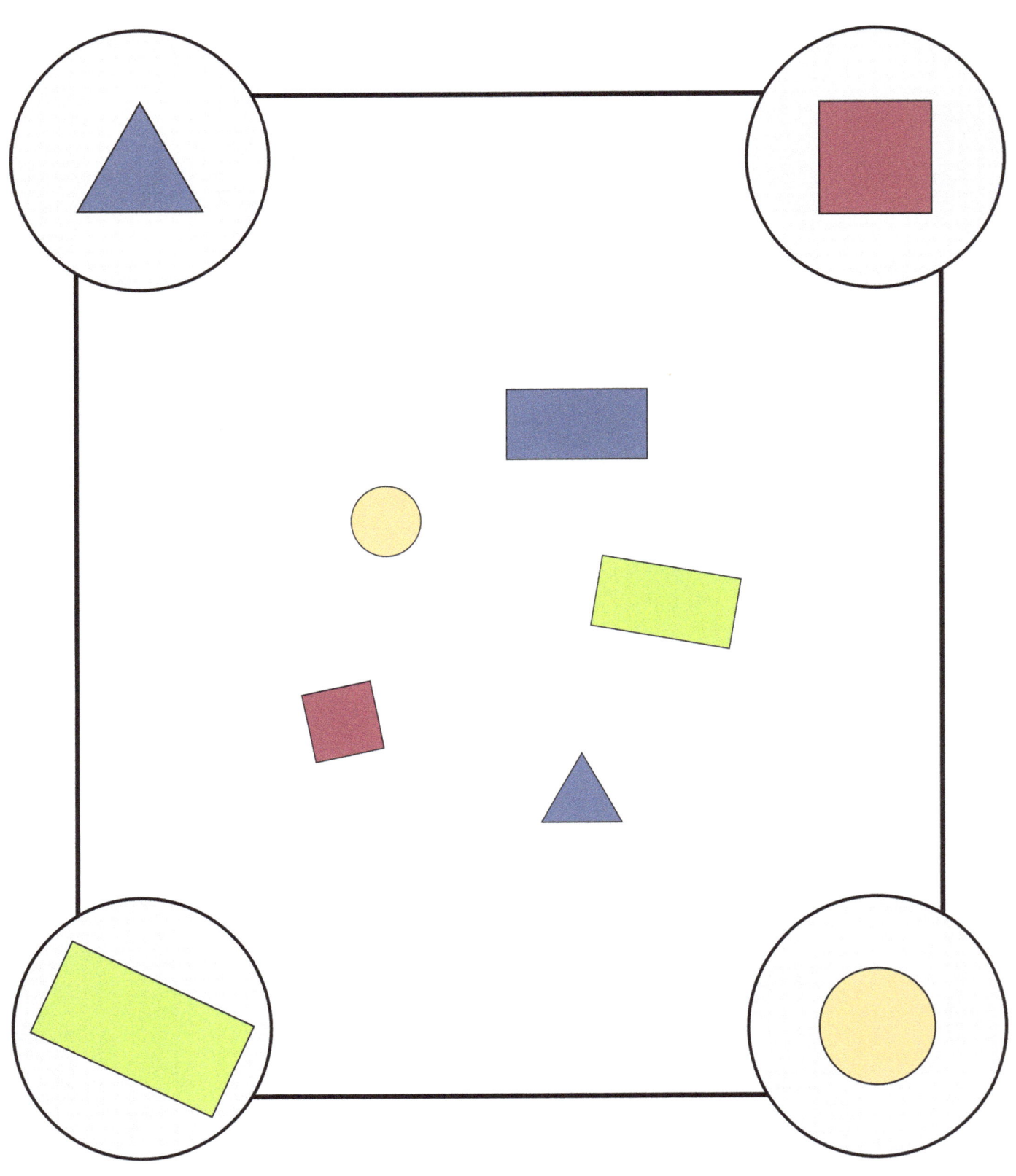

Find **4** Same

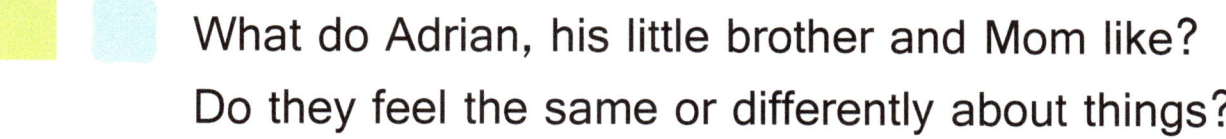

What do Adrian, his little brother and Mom like?
Do they feel the same or differently about things?

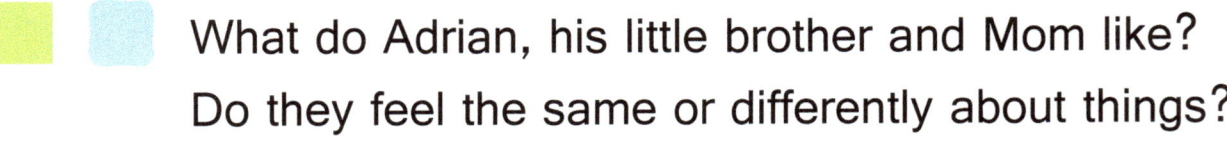

What do Adrian, his little brother and Mom like?
Do they feel the same or differently about things?

What do Adrian, Super-A and Mom like?
Do they feel the same or differently about things?

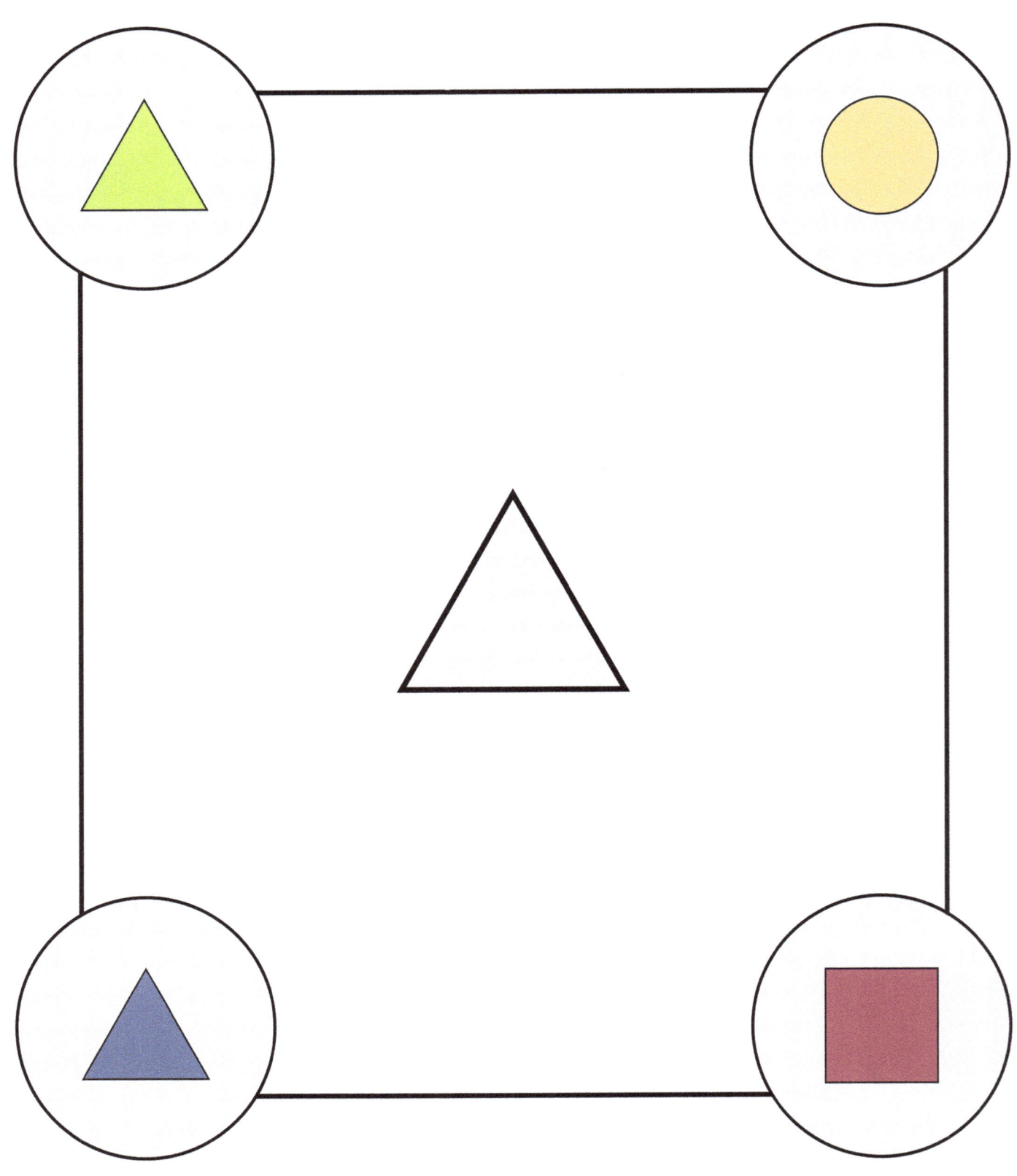

Find 2 Same

It is time to eat! Who likes the bottle?
How many bottles do they need to prepare?

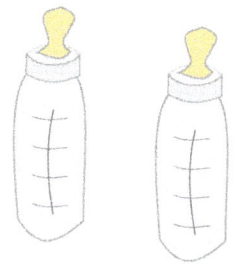 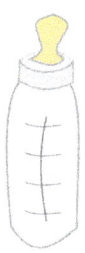 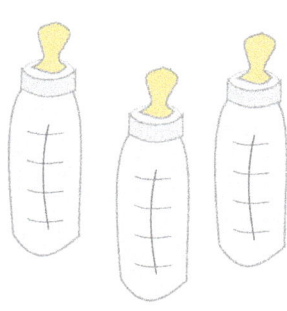

Not everybody is thirsty. Who would like to drink?
How many glasses do they need?

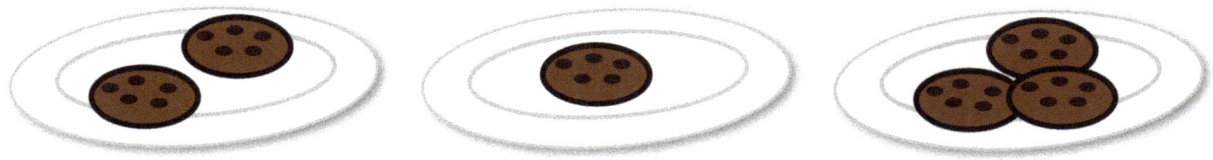 It is cookie time! Who would like a cookie?
How many cookies do they need today?

Find 5 BL●CKS To Build

FIRST → THEN

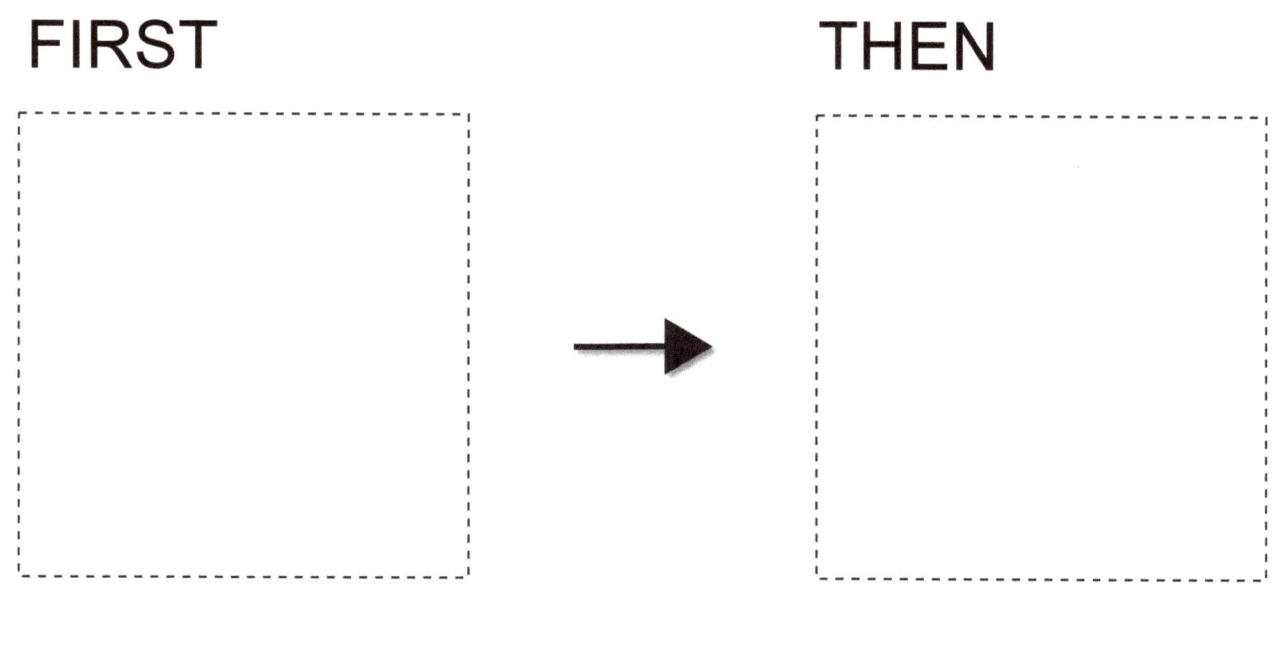

■ We ... wash hands ... whisk eggs ... bake ... drink ... eat cookies ... draw ...   What is first?

(Cut out the page with memory cards. Play memory – order each new pair.)

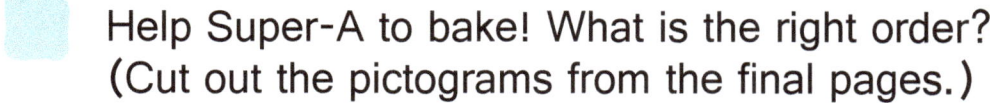

■ Help Super-A to bake! What is the right order?
(Cut out the pictograms from the final pages.)

[1] [2] [3]

Who do you think likes cookies?
Place the persons under the happy or sad smiley.
(Use Adrian and Super-A book characters on next page.)

Cut-outs for the exercises. Above: Order pictograms.
Below: Who likes it? Add your own photos. Place a circle on top of the cookies on the previous page. Explain why you like eggs or soap.

 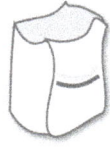   

Soap   Sugar   Coconut   Cookies (coconut macaroon)   iPad

Do you want to get to know Adrian and Super-A better?
There are more workbooks and books!

STARTERS Bake & Like with Adrian and Super-A: Life Skills for Kids with Autism and ADHD
STARTERS Workbook 1 © Jessica Jensen and Be My Rails Publishing 2021
All Rights Reserved. Please note: Teachers may not copy workbooks for educational purposes.
It is not considered fair use if the copying provides replacements or substitutes of workbooks.
The Adrian and Super-A Workbooks may be laminated and reused for the SAME student.
Pictograms kindly provided by www.sclera.be
ISBN 978-91-981522-2-7

Be My Rails Publishing

www.BeMyRails.com

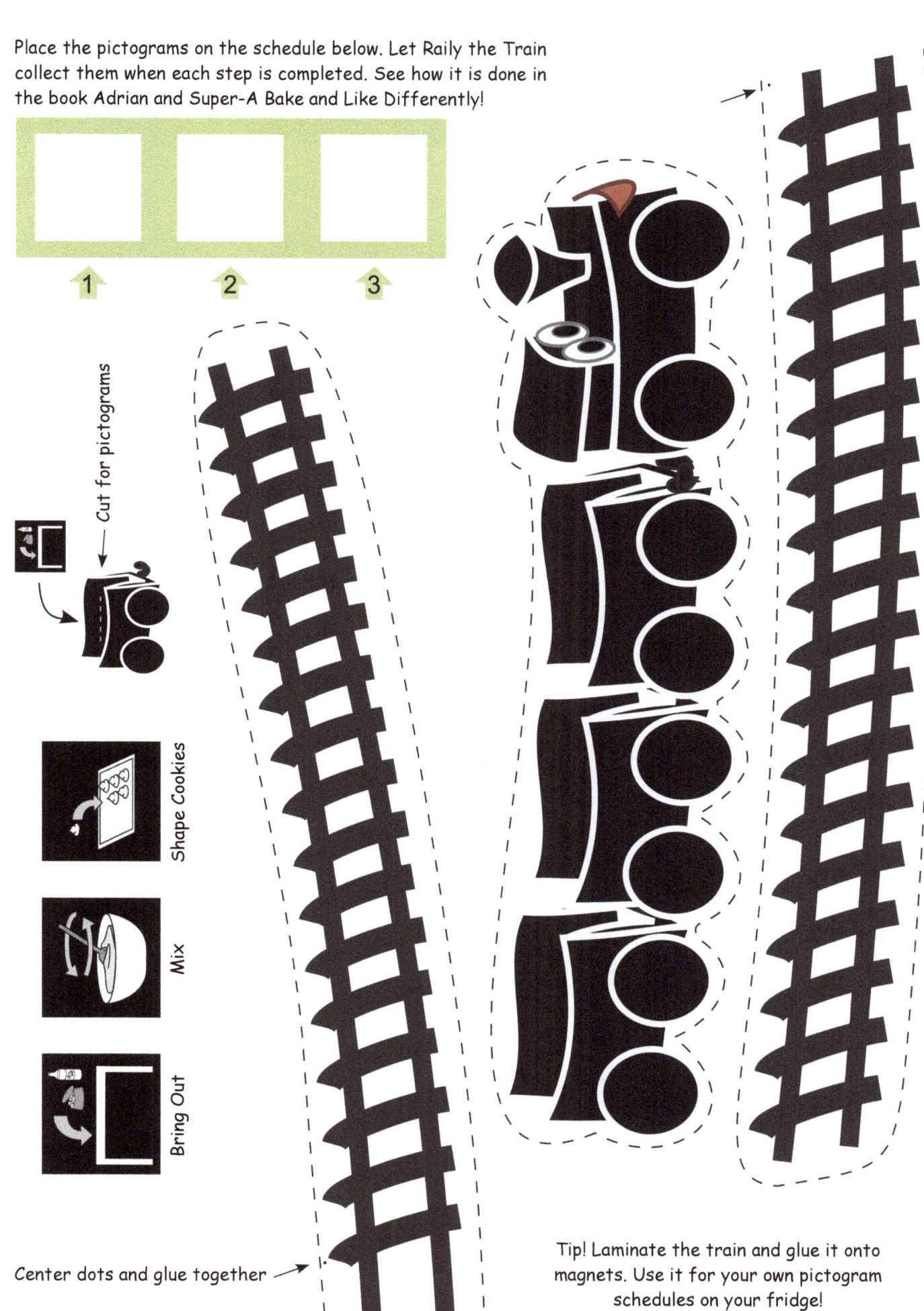